Looking at Minibeasts

Spiders, Centipedes and Millipedes

Morgan

Belitha Press

Contents

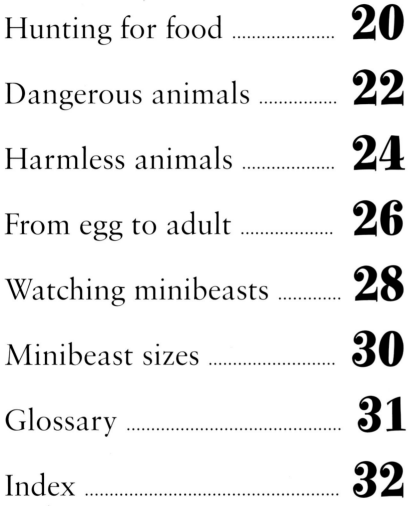

Words in **bold** are
explained on page 31.

What is a spider?

Spiders have eight long legs and eight eyes.

They have strong jaws. A spider's body is

made up of two parts – a head at the front

and an **abdomen**

at the back.

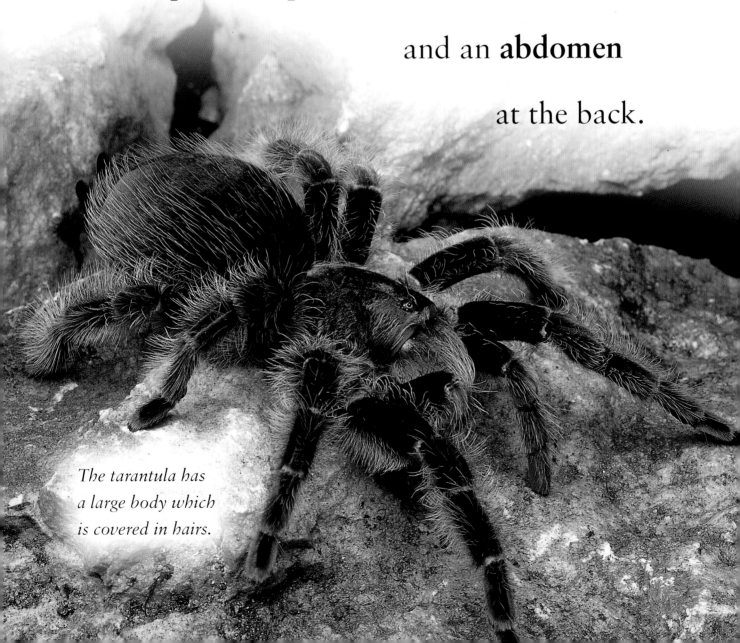

The tarantula has a large body which is covered in hairs.

This spider has two large eyes on the front of its head. The other six eyes look sideways and backwards.

Spiders can be all shapes and sizes. The largest is the bird-eating spider. It lives in rainforests, and can grow to the size of a dinner plate. All spiders use their long legs to run quickly across the ground.

The money spider is one of the smallest spiders.

The spider family

Spiders belong to a group of animals called **arachnids**. They are not **insects**. Scorpions, ticks and mites are arachnids too. The scorpion has a long tail with a **sting** at the end. It has a large pair of powerful claws to grip its **prey**.

The scorpion holds its tail over its body, ready to use its sting.

Mites have eight legs and a large body. This mite is about 3 millimetres long.

Mites and ticks are tiny animals that live on other creatures. They bite through the skin of the animal they live on. Then they feed by sucking the animal's blood.

This tick is living on the body of an animal called a tapir.

Colours and shapes

Many of the spiders we see every day are

a plain brown colour. Some tropical spiders

are brightly coloured. The calico spider has

a body which is coloured orange and black.

*This calico spider is waiting
for prey in the middle
of its web.*

This tarantula is red and black to warn other animals that it has a painful bite.

Some spiders have bright green, **armoured** bodies. Others have heavy, hairy bodies and short legs. The harvestman spider has a small body and very long legs.

You can barely see the long, thin legs of this harvestman spider.

Centipedes and millipedes

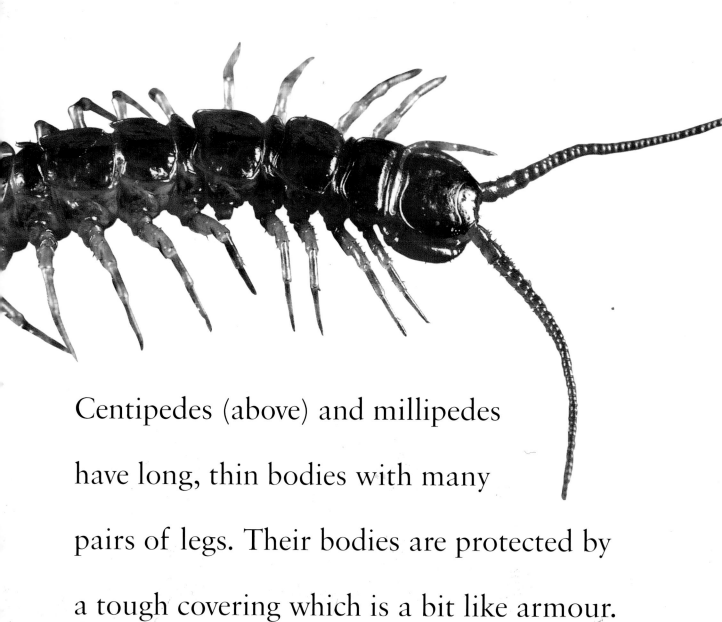

Centipedes (above) and millipedes

have long, thin bodies with many

pairs of legs. Their bodies are protected by

a tough covering which is a bit like armour.

The giant millipede is covered in shiny black and orange armour.

This covering cannot stretch. As the animal grows, it has to **shed** its covering from time to time. The bodies of centipedes and millipedes are made up of many parts called **segments**.

Millipedes have two eyes, two feelers and powerful jaws.

Hundreds of legs

The word millipede means 1000 legs. Millipedes have lots of legs, but they do not have 1000!

The largest millipedes have several hundred legs.

Some tropical millipedes have bright red legs.

There are two pairs of legs on each segment.

The red legs of a giant millipede look like a fringe sticking out from beneath its armoured body.

The word centipede means 100 legs, but centipedes can have between 34 and 250 legs. They have two legs attached to each segment of their bodies – one leg on each side.

This centipede has a pair of legs on each segment of its body.

Fast and slow

Spiders can run quickly on their eight legs. Their sudden movements scare some people.

Each leg is made up of several sections, which are joined together. A spider can bend each leg at these **joints**.

Millipedes cannot move quickly. They crawl along with slow, wavy movements.

In real life, an African millipede is as long as this picture.

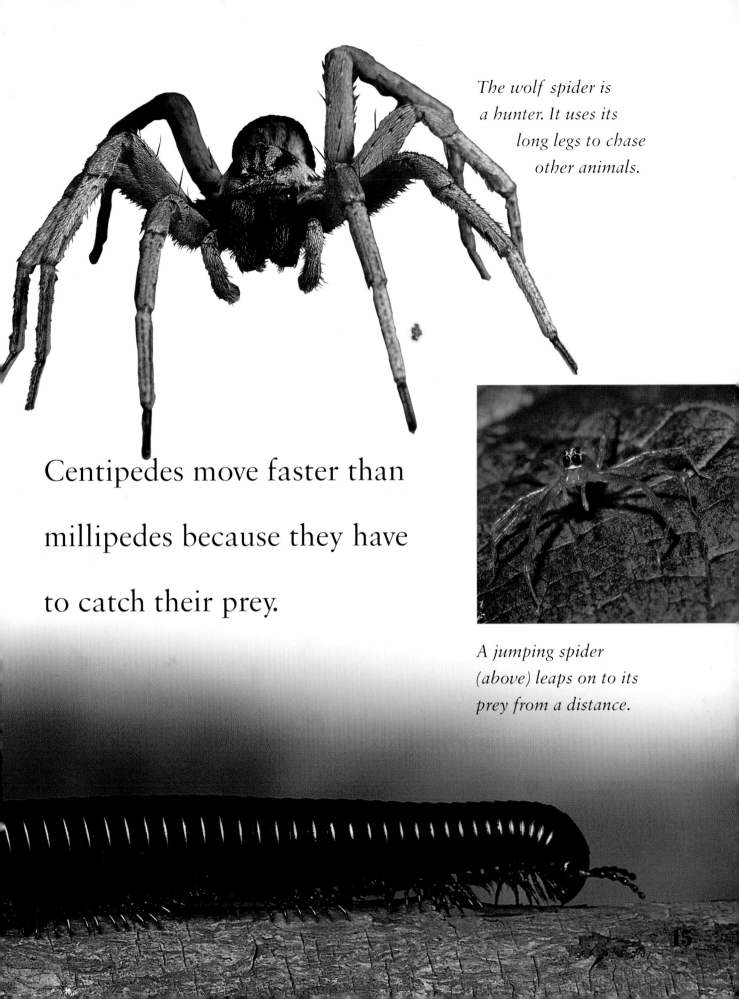

The wolf spider is a hunter. It uses its long legs to chase other animals.

Centipedes move faster than millipedes because they have to catch their prey.

A jumping spider (above) leaps on to its prey from a distance.

Spinning webs

Many spiders spin a web to catch their food.

The web is made from very strong threads

of **silk**. Some of the threads are sticky.

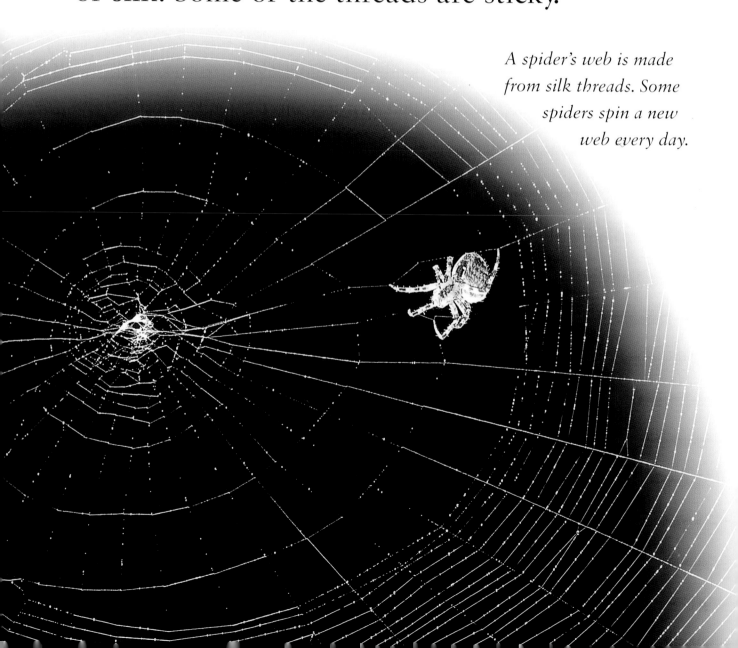

A spider's web is made from silk threads. Some spiders spin a new web every day.

*This spider is pushing out silk
from the back of its abdomen.*

The spider waits in the middle of its web. An insect which flies into the web gets trapped on the sticky threads. The web moves as the insect struggles to escape. This tells the spider that dinner is ready! A spider can catch as many as 100 insects in its web every day.

A spider wraps up an insect in a bundle of silk, and then leaves the insect until it is hungry.

Web styles

There are many different types of spider's webs. The garden spider spins a large spiral web. Some spiders spin a web that looks like a sheet on the ground. It's ideal for catching insects that crawl and hop. A water spider traps air in its web, and then breathes the air when it is underwater.

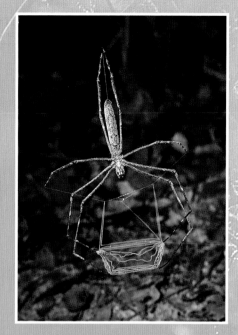

The net-throwing spider makes a small, sticky web to throw over its prey.

A jumping spider sits in the middle of its web, waiting for prey.

19

Hunting for food

Spiders and centipedes are hunting animals. They are called **carnivores**. This means that they feed on other animals. Not all spiders spin webs to catch their prey. The trapdoor spider lives in a burrow in the ground. It makes a trap by spinning out long threads.

The wolf spider sits on a leaf, waiting for a small animal to pass by.

This green lynx spider is hiding inside the leaf of a plant, ready to jump out.

When an insect stumbles over the trap, the spider leaps out and grabs it.

Centipedes are fast-running animals. They catch woodlice, slugs and insects.

This centipede has caught a cockroach in its powerful jaws.

Dangerous animals

Centipedes and spiders have jaws which inject a **poison** into the bodies of their prey. Sometimes, the poison kills the animal at once. Other poisons **paralyse** the

A funnel web spider uses its jaws to inject a poison that can kill large animals.

animal. This means that the prey is still alive, but cannot move its body.

This wandering spider (above) has caught a small frog.

The bite of some spiders, such as the black widow, is so poisonous that it can kill a human.

You can see one of the large jaws of this centipede, between its head and its first leg.

Harmless animals

Millipedes are **herbivores**. This means that they only eat plants. They use their jaws to chew leaves or wood. You can often find them in rotting logs and under the bark of dead trees.

A giant millipede eats fallen leaves on the forest floor.

When a millipede is attacked, it protects itself by curling up into a coil.

Some millipedes can squirt out a liquid that tastes nasty. The liquid puts off any animals that try to attack the millipede.

The body of a giant pill millipede is protected by heavy armour.

From egg to adult

A spider lays up to 800 eggs. The eggs are laid together in a ball. They are protected by a layer of yellow **silk**. After a few weeks, baby spiders hatch from the eggs. These tiny **spiderlings** grow quickly. They **shed** their skin to grow larger.

A female spider wraps up its eggs in silk.

Miniature spiders hatch from the eggs. Each spider is just a few millimetres long.

A centipede lays its eggs one at a time. Each egg is covered with a sticky liquid so that it sticks to the soil. Tiny baby centipedes hatch from the eggs.

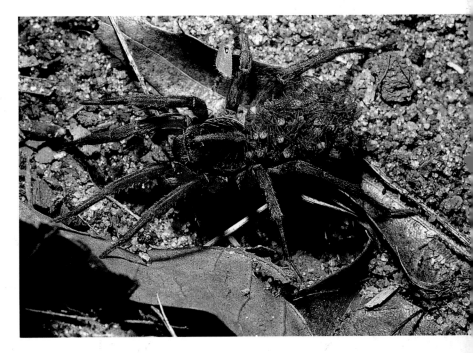

A wolf spider carries its babies on its back for a few weeks after they hatch.

Watching minibeasts

You can find spiders almost anywhere, indoors and out. They are difficult to keep, so it is best to watch them in the wild. Try looking for a spider's web after rain or frost, when the silk threads shine with water. Draw the patterns of the webs you find. If you watch garden spiders closely, you may see them trap their prey. Centipedes and millipedes live under rotting logs and bark, and among dead leaves. A compost heap is a good place to look for them.

A damp, shady log pile is often home to spiders, centipedes, millipedes and other minibeasts.

You can find lots of minibeasts among soil and dead leaves.

Ask a parent or teacher to help you collect some soil and dead leaves. Tip some out on to a large sheet of white paper.

Use a magnifying glass to watch any minibeasts you find. The paper makes it easier to spot them as they run around. Make sure you return all the leaves and animals to the place you found them.

You can buy large, hissing millipedes in a pet shop. They are harmless, noisy animals which can be kept in an old fish tank.

Hissing millipedes like to eat lettuce leaves. Put a layer of soil, leaves and twigs on the bottom of their tank.

Minibeast sizes

Spiders, centipedes and millipedes are many sizes. The pictures in this book do not show them at their actual size. Below you can see how big they are in real life.

Money spider
3-5 millimetres long

Common centipede
30 millimetres long

Calico spider
90 millimetres long

Tarantula
up to 150 millimetres long

Velvet mite
3 millimetres long

Glossary

abdomen The rear part of a spider's body.

arachnid An animal with eight legs, such as a spider.

armoured Covered with a strong, hard case.

carnivore An animal that eats other animals.

herbivore An animal that only eats plants.

insect An animal with six legs and three parts to its body.

joint The place where two parts of a limb are joined. Limbs can bend at a joint.

paralyse To stop an animal from being able to move its muscles.

poison A harmful substance.

prey Animals that are killed by other animals for food.

segment One part of a body.

shed To get rid of something naturally, such as skin or hair.

silk Thin, strong threads made by a spider.

sting The part of an animal that squirts out poison.

spiderling A baby spider.

Index

Editor: Russell McLean
Designers: John Jamieson, Ian Butterworth
Picture researcher: Sally Morgan
Educational consultant: Emma Harvey

First published in the UK in 2000 by
Belitha Press Limited
an imprint of Chrysalis Books plc
64 Brewery Road, London N7 9NT

Paperback edition first published in 2002

ISBN 1 84138 168 3 (hardback)
ISBN 1 84138 392 9 (paperback)

Printed in Hong Kong

British Library Cataloguing in Publication Data
for this book is available from the British Library.

10 9 8 7 6 5 4 3 2 1 (hardback)
10 9 8 7 6 5 4 3 2 1 (paperback)

Picture acknowledgements:
W. Lawlor/Ecoscene: 15t. Raymond Mendez/OSF: 21b.
Sally Morgan/Ecoscene: 8, 30br. Papilio: front & back
cover tcr, 1, 4, 6, 9t, 9c, 14-15, 19br, 26, 30cl.
Jean Preston-Mafham/Premaphotos: 21t.
Ken Preston-Mafham/Premaphotos: front cover tcl, tr,
cl, b; back cover tcl & tr, 3t, 3b, 5t, 7b, 11t, 12, 13t, 15c,
19tr, 22, 23t, 24, 25t, 25b, 27t, 30cr.
Rod Preston-Mafham/Premaphotos: 23b, 27b. Barrie Watts:
front & back cover tl, 2, 11b, 13b, 16, 17t, 17b, 18-19, 20.
Robin Williams/Ecoscene: 5b, 7t, 10, 30bl & tr.